# Tapestry of Inspired Poetry

## by

James A. Pocza

Bloomington, IN  authorHOUSE®  Milton Keynes, UK

AuthorHouse™
1663 Liberty Drive, Suite 200
Bloomington, IN 47403
www.authorhouse.com
Phone: 1-800-839-8640

AuthorHouse™ UK Ltd.
500 Avebury Boulevard
Central Milton Keynes, MK9 2BE
www.authorhouse.co.uk
Phone: 08001974150

First published by AuthorHouse
2/16/2007

ISBN: 978-1-4259-8875-3 (e)
ISBN: 978-1-4259-8874-6 (sc)

Library of Congress Control Number: 2007900344

Printed in the United States of America
Bloomington, Indiana

This book is printed on acid-free paper.

# DEDICATION

Inspired by my wife, family, friends and fellow writers/ poets, who have helped me stretch beyond the norm of everyday life to be seen in a different Light and to share this Light with all.

For the tireless editing and proofing of these penned words I give thanks to my beloved wife, Jeanne.

May all those who have chosen to read these pages of poems be inspired to be

*Spiritually Entwined in Peace, Love and Joy*

*My blessing to each and everyone of you is that you receive the wishes of your lips, the desires of your heart and that you be filled with much Peace, Love and Joy everyday of your life.*

Original Edition: "Tapestry of Inspired Poetry"


By:
James A. Pocza, a.k.a. Plantation 2006
National Poet Laureate @Poets.com

# Quote from a German poet/philosopher Goethe:

*Until one is committed, there is hesitancy, the chance to draw back, always ineffectiveness. Concerning all acts of initiative (and creation), there is one elementary truth the ignorance of which kills countless ideas and splendid plans, that the movement one definitely commits oneself, then providence moves too.*

*All sorts of things occur to help one that would never otherwise have occurred. A whole stream of events issue from the decision, raising in one's favor all manner of unforeseen incidents and meetings and material assistance, which no man could have dreamed would have come his way.*

*Whatever you can do or dream you can, begin, boldness has genius, power and magic in it.*

*Begin it now.*

This inspiring quote of Goethe was the catalyst that challenged me to write poems/cinquains and to publish this book to which I am ever grateful.

*James A. Pocza, a.k.a. Plantation,*
*National Poet Laureate @Poet.com*

## To the reader.........

I am a diverse poetry writer. If one line, stanza or poem speaks to your heart, and allows you to ponder, I have accomplished my goal.

# TABLE OF CONTENTS

## Selection 1 Diverse Poetry Contents

# Selection 2 Cinquain Contents

# Selection 1
# Diverse Poetry Contents

# Section 1 Diverse Poetry

"Poetry always aims to please by the presentation of that which is beautiful. All real poetry produces an aesthetic effect by appealing to our aesthetic sense; that is, to our love of the beautiful."

Quote by Stratton D. Brooks, 1905

## PENNILESS ANGELS (Example)

Penniless Angels ride the soft clouds
Gratis

Like poet Doves of Earth who pen words
Gratis

Words descending like angel dust
Gratis

Enlightening our hearts and minds
Gratis

Waves of words to feed creativity
Gratis

All given in love/received from above
Gratis

Author's Comments:
*"Inspiration can come at any given moment like this write was given in love."*

# CHAPTER 1. INSPIRATION

# Candle Of A Man

*To my Dad and the Man who was in his life and now is mine.*

Dear God above, You who are Infinite, can make the sky so blue, the grass so green, and the water so cool and clear, can take from this land a person, a being, You created in the likeness of Yourself and give him everlasting life. In a Palace that no mortal man could ever attempt to duplicate here on this Earth. A Palace that holds eternal life for all who have been so near and dear to Him.

Life, like a burning candle, glows for many years for some, while others are needed above to carry out His wishes. Their candle burns out swiftly, like a sudden gust of wind.

That candle, candle of a man, filled with a once ever bursting flame, a bright shining light and a warmth of comfort. Now his candle burns slightly lower. Flicker, flicker, goes the light of that once tall proud, humble, shinning candle of a man until it flickers no more.

That candle, candle of a man, comes forth with a burst of flame, lit again to lead us through our hours of darkness. Never once flickering in our time of need. Instead that tall, proud, humble, candle of a man holds steady that ever amber glow of life and love.

Silent now, but stronger than ever could be expressed by mortal words. You can't caress it, squeeze it, or hold it, but it is yours to cherish until once again you light that special candle, candle of a man; Jesus, the light of man.

FAITHFUL TRUE LOVE FOREVER

Author's Comments:
*"A father's love endures forever as my father's love remains with me in time of need."*

# SOWING OUR SEEDS

By Your grace, my Lord and my God, grant us:
Wisdom
Knowledge
Understanding
Fruits of Your Spirit
We ask for these gifts in abundance as we go
about sowing our seeds, singing praises to You.

We give glory to your holy name in thanksgiving
for our new life. We remain open with humility and openness
to the Holy Spirits promptings of love, joy peace, and gentleness

Help us as your people to extend seeds of love perpetually
to all our brothers and sisters. Heal us by forgiving
and forgetting each other's faults.

Thank you for listening, Jesus, and harboring us in your love.
For Your mercy endures forever. Speak Lord your servant listens.

Amen, come Lord Jesus

# There Is A Balm

*To all in need of healing*

Could it be the RING?
Or the oil of GLADNESS
How about the ROSE?
Then there is LOVE

There is pure SUNSHINE
Warming close HUGS
A pleasant smile SHINES
PETAL soft lips to KISS

A fragrant large HIBISCUS
Colorful in glory MAGNOLIA
Forget not the PUSSY WILLOW
Whispering aqua DROPLETS

All these and more HEAL
You have tried the REST
When all else FAILS
JESUS is the BEST

Author's Comments:
*"No real rhyme or reason just reflecting on
different long lasting healing supplements."*

# Tranformation

*T o a very special Angel who loves me unconditionally*

I stood upon a fluffy white cloud
Before the Almighty I bowed
I had no fear in looking down
Only joy I found as I looked around

Wonderful Sunshine and Bluest skies
Brought tears flowing from my eyes
Such silence, I've never known before
Calm and peace there at heavens door

Oceans of love poured and surged
A joyful loving spirit emerged
A complete transformation inside of me
You are my son, in my image then be

Go now and descend in new robe of white
You are my light amongst all men
Let your light shine both day and night
I am with you always, in all ways, amen

I said, "So be it, and Amen."

Author's Comments:
*"This a very special experience I had in meditation.
Yes, there are Angels all around us, mine lives and talks with me
daily."*

# THE LORD'S PRE NATAL FLOAT

*To all who love unconditionally*

I remember being safe, in the cozy womb.
My Mom was carrying me, into a little room.
No Daddy I heard, or could be found.
Alone in the dark, I heard a sound.

Loud noises now, I want to spout.
Eyes closed, unhappy about to pout.
Doctor probing me, I may be a preemie,
Yippee, I cried, I could come out early.

Two months premature, I've been told.
A little boy, blue, skinny, crying, cold.
I got my first spanking, lungs so strong
although underweight, nothing was wrong.

Years later, strong, and healthy were I.
I questioned the Lord, were you not standing by?
When I was struggling, and turning blue.
HE said I was the water in the womb that carried you.


Author's Comments:
*"To any person, child or adult who doubts there is a God,*
*He is with you always in all ways."*

# Percentages

*To all seeking inner wisdom and truth*


What we can see and feel
Is only a small percentage we conceal
A deeper depth to plunge
Of what really is going on inside

of us

Like an Iceberg there is another resolve
Depth to see and melt within many
as the inner healing and melting dissolve
takes place sadness is replaced by joy

of us

The possibility of greatness within exist
Will come forth in each and everyone's midst
A new vibrant flow of energy
Begins to flow and fills all

of us

Then your imagination will perceive
what no longer will be allowed to deceive
that what is below in our subconscious
A new freedom will emerge in all

of us

Then your spirit will be free to soar

Author's Comments:
*"The essence of imagination dwells many times
below the surface of our inner being and mind."*

# Four Cornerstones

*To all who are builders of HIS Kingdom*

Each corner has a special stone
and every stone a special place
Neither which can stand alone
and each must have its perfect place

The first shall not be last one laid
Nor shall the last be laid before
Faith, Hope, Love and Charity weighed
These then most precious of the four

All of four stones we should applaud
Our lives then paved with perfect trust
Each stone a symbol of the Lord
Foundations set in place for us

Nor of the stones are guilt and sorrow
but part of what life seems to bring
So place your stones with Faith tomorrow
Then praise and thank our heavenly King.


Author's Comments:
"Inspired by my beloved, and the many poets
who share the Love of the same Lord."

# BREATHLESS

*To all His chosen children*

A muted
Voice

A perfect
Act

Evidence of
Belief

Breathe in His
Spirit

Exhale His
Love

Live in
Peace

Sing and dance in
Joy

Be breathless in
Jesus


Author's Comments:
"A morning inspiration as I drew in my first
conscious breath that I wanted to share with all."

# As The Good Lord Intended
# (Free Verse)

*To those seeking the way of the Lord*

Passing quickly by, witnessing events of someone else's tragedy,
many times without as much as a small prayer being uttered.

Witness's passing by or rushing to view a nearby house fire. We become
un-threatened observers, onlookers, of someone else's devastation.

I am certain others have witnessed our own tragedies on our road of life,
with the same detached feelings as those of these observers.

We maintain an ordered externalization of our own fears and anxieties
that keep us in private nightmares.

We must purge these negative thoughts by rubbernecking our own life to
a full stop after slowing down.
Past mistakes and tragedies we have suffered,
to no longer affect our feelings or future.

The answer is not to repeat the same mistakes, instead to
enjoy the new tomorrow, the new experiences and the
richness and rewards of life in " Him "... our beloved Lord.

Only then are we truly able to feel another's pain and suffering.
Only then, can we become the helper and not just the observer.
Only then can we all become as the Lord intended.....Amen.

Author's Comments:
*"The Joy of the Lord is within, seek and you shall find."*

# Bathtub Miracle
# (Free Verse)

*To my wife, children, family, friends and poet friends*

There was a time for me when all hell broke loose
while in the military where I served on foreign soil.
I acquired a germ called Malaria. Pills, pills none
of these given healed me. It was also established

I had contacted "Jungle Rot" on both feet and toes.
The flesh on my toes was slowly being eaten away
over an 18-year period of time. Working many long
hard hours and at the same time serving the Lord
and His people in my church with a pain and stench
from feet that was very putrid. Only known to my
family and children and very close friends.

One day after work and having some extra time before
my evening church meeting, I took a much-needed
slow relaxing tub bath. Feet propped up out of the
water, for the water created sharp pains on toes.

Not to test the Lord, but I asked a question.
"Jesus, am I really walking and doing what you want
me to do in your church? " Suddenly, a couple of tears
trickled down my cheeks from both eyes. I quickly
wiped them dry and removed myself from the bathtub.

Seating myself to pat dry my feet and toes, I felt my
towel was not hurting my feet as usual to wipe,
I began sobbing and sobbing out loud, for both
my feet were instantly healed, PRAISE THE LORD!

At the same time a scripture passage was given to
me that I heard in Spirit, ISAIAH 52:7.
"How beautiful upon the mountains are the feet
of him who brings good news." AMEN AND AMEN.

Author's Comments: "Just one of the many miracles I have
received from the Lord.
Peace, Love and Joy be with all who read this. P.S. I love going
barefooted now !!!"

# CHALICE OF LOVE
## (FREE VERSE)

*To all believers and non-believers hoping*

My first nourishing drink was within my mother's womb
Second drink after spanked was of my first breath
Mother's warm breast milk was the first Chalice I drank from
The chalice that held holy water was sprinkled upon my head

Fully baptized I was blessed with all the gifts everyone receives
I drank from the Chalice of His blood at my first communion
There after for many youthful years I partook of this blessing
The military afforded me this blessing even on foreign soil

I was extended this same Chalice of Love to me at my marriage
My thirst continued as I served others with this Chalice of Love
Containing the wine believers know to be the blood of Jesus
Life is short, but not in heaven, drink now from this Chalice of
Love

Upon the clouds of forgiveness I shall thirst and shed tears
My desire is to drink from His Chalice of Love in eternity
Standing in wait holding my empty Chalice of Love
Amen, come Lord Jesus and fill my Chalice of Love to the brim

Author's Comments:
*"The pure Peace, Love and Joy is in the Lord only."*

# Rubbernecking
## (Free Verse)

To those seeking the way of the Lord

Passing quickly by witnessing events of someone else's tragedy,
Many times without as much as a small prayer being uttered.

Witness's passing by or rushing to view a nearby house fire.
We become un-threatened observers, onlookers, of someone
else's devastation.

I am certain other have witnessed our own tragedies on our road
of life,
with the same detached feelings as those of these observers.

We maintain an ordered externalization of our own fears
and anxieties that keep us in private nightmares.

We must purge these negative thoughts by rubbernecking our own
life and slowing down.  Past mistakes and tragedies we have
suffered,
to no longer affect our feelings or future.

The answer is not to repeat the same mistakes, instead to enjoy
the new tomorrow, the new experiences and the richness and
rewards
of life in "Him"…our beloved Lord.

Only then are we truly able to feel another's pain and suffering.
Only then, can we become the helper and not just the observer.
Only then can we become as the Lord intended…..Amen


Author's comments:
"The Joy of the Lord is within, seek and you shall find."

# THE SPARK

Ignited the living flame of love

Touched by the Divine Dove

My hands were lightly caressed

Sealed with kiss of love I am blessed


A cold heart melted quickly away

Upon my knees I did not sway

Flame of love now extending

Your turn my friend I am not pretending


Reach up and be open to love

He stands at the door of your heart

He will send you His own Dove

From the start He shall not depart


Author's Comments:

"It will only take a small spark to ignite His flame of love."

# Flight/Fright Is Over

To all surviving family members, friends of that heroic flight.

A chilling crisp clear September morn
Passengers boarded the flight for a distant destination
Happiness was abound as the lift off was smooth
Glancing out the window many saw leaves adorned

Early Fall leaves showing their beginning glory
Dew drops of moisture still on the leaves
Was trickling down upon each descending lower leaf
Each awaiting hungrily the next nourishing droplet to fall

Soon these sights will vanish from their sight
The clouds seen now were soft as white puffy cotton
The Pilot announced over the speakers, we have been hijacked.
All terrified, yet calm, they began their prayers and phone calls

Because of their unselfish desire to overcome adversity
The terrorist threat was squashed, and a larger disaster plot was
diverted
Two charging words still are heard in our hearts and minds
Generations and nations shall remember, these shouted words

"Lets roll"

The unsung now sung heroes for years to come.
All 40 passengers, Pilot and crewmembers on
Flight 93 arrived at Heaven, Gate One

ON TIME….September 11, 2001

Author's Comments:
*"This write was inspired by recent visit to the temporary memorial.*
*By His Grace, we give our humble Gratitude.*
*There names are now preserved on sacred ground*
*who showed the power of Faith, Hope and unselfish Love*
*possible in the face of death."*

# Laborers Needed

*ATTN: Hiring now for all Eternity*

The harvest is greater than all past years
Hard work, great pay, no tears
All applications will be accepted
regardless of gender or religion

Past work history not checked
No drug, alcohol tests, smokers OK
Bankrupts forgiven, liberal dress code
Bad credit rating, no problem A-ONE, now

Any and all sins forgiven
Guilt will not be tolerated
Fear to join is not an option
Long hours, low pay, high rewards

Job description; Desire to witness
to the undying love of Jesus
Many are called few are chosen
Your job is to call and to forgive

Author's Comments:

*"Hours are long 24/7's, 365 days a year.
Can I count on you to show up on time? "*

# Penniless Angels

*To: All poets round the world*

Penniless Angels ride the soft clouds
Gratis

Like poet Doves of Earth who pen words
Gratis

Words descending like angel dust
Gratis

Enlightening our hearts and minds
Gratis

Waves of words to feed creativity
Gratis

All given in love/received from above
Gratis

Author's Comments:

*"Inspiration can come at any given moment like
this write was given in love."*

## "Spiritual Junkies"

What is on the table?

Seeking to get my fill of enlightment
Feeling like I am in total disarray
Searching, longing for truth not disorder
Never asking to receive, always stumbling

Each smorgasbord filled with pamphlets
Nothing to dine on sprinkled with wine droplets
Onward to another table filled fruits of love
Moving around in a circle seeking amour

Tried Yoga, meditation, Tai Chi to no avail
Then came the people at the home door
All they asked of me, am I spiritually awake
Yes, and many times I have given to the poor

Will I accept Jesus as my personal Savior?
Yes, yes and yes for all times I will
I won't receive a bill; in full He paid the bill
No more a " Spiritual Junkie," I am saved.


Author's comments:
AMEN, AMEN HALLELUJAH

# WAKE UP
# (FREE VERSE)

To sons and daughters who have gone fishing
with their Dad.

Wake up son, the fish are biting
Lets go now before dawn breaks
I got the minnows you get the worms
Don't forget the lunches Mom packed

Dad, how far do we have to travel?
Not far, first we must rent a boat
Did Jesus have to travel this early?
Yes, and He took His disciples with Him

There is a slight wind to keep us cool
Is the water going to be rough? No
Jesus stood in a boat and calmed the wind
Will He be with us if it gets to rough? Yes

Why do we need fishing poles, Jesus didn't?
Jesus said, to cast a net, do we have net?
No, son we do not, but He is always with us
I hope you catch a big fish for dinner, son

I thought we are supposed to fish for men?
How do we fish for men?
First you tell everyone of His love
Then you say fear and guilt are not of Him

He spoke truth and performed miracles
Many believed and you will some day
I do now Dad, and I have been saved
Have you been saved? Yes, PRAISE THE LORD!!

Author's Comments:

*"Out of the mouth of Babes come precious questions."*

23

# Be On Guard

*To all of us tempted in so many ways*


He speaks and many listen...
His eyes didn't even glisten

Words spoken were to seduce...
Falling in to his commanding glance

Pole dance... NO WAY, unless I am in a trance
Showed me lots of money if I would dance

Then I remembered...Jesus is not a tempter
I called upon His name and blood, fled the tempter

Quickly... was I released ran to my home
Upon my knees I gave thanks in my abode

Beware... of the wolf in sheep's clothing
Be it man or woman both prowl and prey

Jesus said," know I am with you in all ways."
"You shall not perish, I am with you always."


Author's Comments:

*"Keep the FAITH, and be filled with
Peace, Love and Joy*

# BRAIDED LOVE

Seek and you shall find and He will answer you.

The Master Braider looked down
There was upon my face a frown

You need a mate to charm
Walk beside you arm in arm

No more pool of dreams to dance to
For I shall make you permanently two

The two shall become one
Never fear I will not be out done

Two souls I will especially braid
Destiny written upon each plaited

You are mine filled with love
I shall always be your only Dove

Call upon me when you are unbraided
I AM only a brush away to have you re-plaited

Author's Comments:
*"The depth of His love is unending."*

# Log In, Log Out

Words of wisdom

Turn it on and log in and wait
Turn it off and more time to wait
Perceive the time the computer takes
How do you spend the time it takes?

At it again, daily turning it on
Must check emails before moving on
No time for past friends
They have tunnel vision my friends

Jesus said, "First you must take the log out
of your own eye,
before you can take the speck out
of your brother's eye."

Time now to log in and on to the Lord
His lap-top is always available never bored
No waiting for log in time, never a log out
All logs and specks will be taken out

Author's comments:

*"The more we seek in others, the more we don't
see in ourselves the log."*

# CHAPTER 2. LOVE/ROMANCE

# Come Up My Love

*To all who are united in marriage, love and Spirit*

I shall find you, do not dread
Even amongst brambles
Your cry I have heard
Not to leave you in shambles

You are eternally mine
Our vows spiritually read
We will Heavenly dine
A heavy heart not to dread

I know all your fears
I've had some fears too
When your eyes weep those tears
I will pat them dry for you

I'm there for your rescue
Need not rope or winch
Weep not and hold on to me
Whatever it takes I'll not flinch

I'll always be there for you
So assured you can rest
I'm there for your rescue
Red Rover never to fear is best

Author's Comments:

*"Where ever our lovers are we will rescue them in the
name of Love. True love will be had by all."*

# Spin The Bottle

*To children who ever played the game and found love*

Randomly the bottle pointed
As I sat crossed leg'd hoping
Anxiously feeling disjointed
Waiting my turn, I was coping

The bottle began to spin
She sat there looking endearing
Girl, white dress and gold hairpin
I prayed my turn was nearing

Ocean blue eyes sparkled at me
A pink sash at her waist
The bottle began to spin again
Such agony now I faced

In torment I sat waiting my turn
And watching this vision of bliss
As she watched me her heart did yearn
For the magic of our first kiss

The bottle it then stopped spinning
Never to stop upon us two
Now feeling rejected for not winning
I knew what I had to do

Turning toward the sweet beauty
Brushing her pig tails back gently
I thought it my schoolboy duty
And kissed her with passion aplenty

No childhood game was ever greater
In our memories to ever recall
And who'd have thought twenty years later
We'd kiss once again at a ball

Little blond damsel mine now to hold
And the kisses never to end
What joy I'd missed, If I hadn't kissed
My little blonde schoolgirl friend.

Author's Comments:
*"The first kiss is always the first to remember
and the last one just felt is tenderly remember also.
It will bring sunshine to your heart as it does mine every day."*

# Kiss

*To my wife, Jeanne*

Blow me a kiss, now your sweet kiss
One I know that you won't miss
I always have this deep desire
You and I can rekindle the fire

Tis only you that I adore
Let's hold on forever more
You are the world and more to me
My heart will never set you free

Every moment in this life
Ever proud that you're my wife
Every word for you I write
My star that's ever shining bright

Never more shall I doubt
Nothing more to make me pout
My love awaits yours in return
For you my love I'll ever yearn

Author's Comments:
*"My personal poem to my wife that our love
has continued to grow over the years and
for this I love you."*

# My Angel Wife

An Angel there before my eyes
Oh how I prayed for one like you
This love I feel is no surprise
Such joy you bring in all you do

When you appeared there in my dreams
I asked the Lord to make you mine
My feelings taken to extremes
And then our vows were sealed and signed

And now we are as man and wife
Fulfilled us two in every way
For you and I new lease of life
Upon my knees with thanks each day

# THIS LOVE

*To my wife who is always at my side*


Seeing her in a crowd my heart skipped a beat,
she turned and smiled at me.
I smiled back and our eyes locked for a second;
she then quickly turned and walked away.
I thought I had lost her as the crowd in the
dance hall swelled before my eyes, I was
about to leave when I saw her again talking
to a group of friends, I gingerly walked up
and asked her to dance, a long pause and then
she smiled and accepted my
outstretched hand.

One dance and my heart skipped so fast I
thought I would faint, the smell of her
perfume, her blond hair and ice blue eyes, I was
completely taken as I felt her warm tender body close to mine,
she smiled and gently squeezed my hand to
let me know she was
feeling my desires. We never left the dance floor that night,
every dance was ours.

Many summers have passed but the thrill of that
evening is ever fresh in my mind
and as I look at her now, my wife, my love,
my life, my heart still skips the way it did in that
dance hall all those summers ago.
....Darling I love you.....

# Hide-a-way

*To my beloved*

A special Island of Romance
A place where two beloved's dance
Near a heavenly blue lagoon
Neath a clear sky and full moon

There is not a single teardrop
Angels above sprinkle loving dust
Two loving earthly stars shine
Each entwined saying you are mine

How far they both had traveled
To find such a place to unravel
A travelers delight of accommodations
Where there is love, there is no damnation

Morning Sunshine awakens their love
The singing of a far away dove
A smile of satisfaction upon each their face
Their blue lagoon, a loving place.


Author's Comments:
*"When one finds true love, one wants to write
about that love to the beloved and all."*

# Hibiscus and You (Acrostic)

*To the true flower of my life, my beloved*

Heaven found there within your eyes

Inviting and so divine

Beauty then to take my breath

Intoxicating, like vintage wine.

Sweet you are and ever will be

Chasing clouds on angel wings

Un-dying love for you my queen

Scented Hibiscus and you, love brings

Author's Comments:

*"Beauty is in the eyes of the beholder,
and in each flower of the same essence."*

# CHANTILLY LACE (FICTION)

*A poem for all those who enjoy a little fantasy and romance...*

The arrival of the belle of the ball
Many a man's heart heard to race
She captured the eyes of them all
As she moved with style and grace

The dance hall glowed with her beauty
Not a hair could be seen out of place
Dance card was filling up with suitors
All taken by her beautiful face

When all of a sudden a Prince did appear
So handsome and gallant was he
He eyed the belle and said, excuse me my dear
would you have the next dance with me?

She curtsied, he bowed, and took to the floor
in his arms she had found a safe place
He whispered, and will you be mine, ever more
Oh my beauty, in Chantilly lace?

# ALL OF YOU

*To my beloved who always watches over me*

Such joy and peace you bring to me,
your laughter now, and my food of love.
You clothe me, in such tenderness,
your smile, and a gift from up above.

This home we made, our loving nest.
The beauty of your golden hair.
Sweet poetry you are to me.
No life for me, without you there.

With you I find such happiness,
and, so it comes as no surprise.
That I'm a happy man today,
my love for you, here in my eyes.

Author's Comments:

*"Within the eyes of your beloved you shall see
the reflection of your self. True Love"*

# GARMENTS OF ROMANCE

*To all night time beach walkers and lovers*


Clothed in soft lavender was she tonight
The glamour of a thousand stars
were dwelling in her beautiful eyes just right
Sandals rich as the sand neath her feet

Blue eyes like the depth of the ocean floor.
Yellow reflection of the sunset was bracelet worn.
Smiling face reflecting the joy of the evening.
Rich glow of crimson was the scarf overhead

Warm air of twilight was scented
with the fragrance of sweetbrier.
The washing of the ripples along the shore
could be heard in the silence of the stillness.

Lying upon the exceeding beauty of the twilight
Golden hair length reflecting the last rays of sunlight
Now awaiting her nightly Prince from far away shore
To behold her beauty and her kisses forever more.


Author's Comments:

*"A stroll along the beaches at night finds many a maiden
reflecting / wishing and resting."*

# Did You See That? (Free Verse)

*To: All Romantics*

Behold the front porch sights at night
A shooting star across the sky to the right
Oh, look a little chipmunk scampering
We have a glorious full moon tonight

Lets hold hands again like before
Shall we make a wish upon that star?
Your hands so soft and warm in mine
I feel your tender heart upon my arm

Will you please strum a song tonight?
Look! See the squirrel in the tree over there
and the wild rabbit with both ears up high
both animals' heads swaying while you play

Please play another memory song or two
I love rocking here with you
Front porch sights ending
Time to go inside my dear


Author's Comments:

*"There is a time for everything.
This is just one of those times to look and love."*

# Magnets Of Love

*To all with wishes of their heart's desires for their beloved's*

Magnets are meant to attract and detract
Magnets float if you sprinkle the particles apart
Like magnets we can float apart or be drawn together
Playfully we can attract and also chase each other to depart

Together we make powerful electrifying energy
With particles of love we can draw pictures of love petals
Magnets are used to lift up nuts, bolts and heavy metals
We can use the same human energy to lift each other upward

A numerous host of particles in love must contain
natural ingredients like eyes, smiles, hugs, warmth and retain
equal likes and dislikes couple these all then with truth
There are over 1001 other particles like these to attract

My number one particle that keeps me attracted to love
Is the God of Love, Jesus, sending particles from the Dove
sprinkling on you and me particles of Peace, Love and Joy
He is the perfect magnet for now and all eternity

Author's Comments:

*"What particles do you use to attract others to yourself or Him?"*

# Gale Force Wind (Free Verse)

*To my beloved wife*

A love I never thought possible ended my drought
Swirled and whirled creating an onslaught
Standing my ground until the heated wind subsided
My beloved on that day took me by storm

SHE

Showered me with the Sunshine of her love

SHE

Blessed me with the comfort of her arms

SHE

Turned my nights into days of love

SHE

Calls me now husband, I call her now wife

The Gale Force Wind of July 1999
Has long since been remembered
As a pivotal moment in our lives
That was the day we both said "I Do."

Author's Comments:

*"Remembering"*

# True Love (Free Verse)

*To my beloved*

How wonderful to wake each morning, and look upon
your beautiful face, the sun, streaming though the window,
as if an angel had shone a light on you, laying there.
Tears fill my eyes for the very power of love I feel for you.

Oh my beloved, you who brought such tenderness
into my then empty world. You who took me from
darkness to light with your very first kiss, that I might
never again feel the loneliness that once shrouded
my unhappy life.

Oh that I could take the very stars from the sky
and lay them at your beloved  feet, that you
would then forever walk a heavenly path, filled with
light and love. Oh my beloved that I should
ever wake and find you gone.

Author's Comments:

*"True Love can be found at any age and last forever,
sometimes we just have to wait for its arrival longer
than others have to experience."*

# Ways To Make Love

*Just ideas to enhance love without doing it*

Always tell the person that you love them
Make a special tape or CD of their love songs
Read or write each other poems at night
Dine with flowers and candle light

Give each other pet names like "Bunny"
Flirt with each other with a foot massage
Laugh at something really funny
Dedicate a song on the radio to each other

Bake their favorite, chocolate chip, cookie
Share desired lifetime together goals
Have a picture taken together of your souls
Do things for each other without being asked

Listen to each other's hurts by others that ding
Give or receive a special meaningful ring
Walk arm in arm in the woods or on a beach
Give or get a Hug "O" or a Kiss "X"


Author's Comments:

*"Try it you will like it, Yummy cookies...On second
thought how about telling each other you love them
in different languages?"*

# CHAPTER 3. RELATIONSHIPS

# Special Son (Free Verse)

Came forth as my first born
Loved before he took his first breath
In the womb constant kicking, punching
Amazing features, and saw my own reflection

Early years became a parent's challenge
Never had a book on how to raise him
First steps a clue to where life was leading
Avid reader, travels and loves to entertain

Never a doubt or concern of own ability
Played baseball, kick ball very athletic
From center field to home plate the ball soared
Threw perfect strike, runner out, saved the game

Served his country in the Air Force
Devoted husband with own first-born son now
Believes in his Lord God of love
Charitable, unending giving of heart, time

Educated, self taught in life struggles
Carries his challenges without a whimper
A people person loved by family and friends
Same surname and a father's pride and joy

# "Frenchie"

*To my daughter and her love of her Parakeet*

You gladden my heart and soul.

Always seeing you move with grace.

Knowing you found that seed.

Daring not to tempt an embrace.

Doing everything possible naturally.

IN FRONT OF GOD AND EVERYONE.

Up, down and around you see your reflection.

What was one, now is two.

Somehow you look the same.

All because you see a dame.

You think you love her.

It is I, who love you more.

Your mirror reflects the new you each day.

A real mess you made.

Will you please stop and settle down.

I've tried talking and singing.

I'll bet your ears are ringing.

There that's the way, all done for this day.

Calm as a Cove or a Bay in his cage.

"My Parakeet doesn't know what to say".

Author's Comments:
"Watching my daughter cleaning out her Parakeet's cage
was a joy of a young child's love in taking care of her first pet."

45

# Daddy's Hands

*To all who have or had a Daddy who toils endlessly on their behalf.*

There was always....Love in Daddy's hands
Soft....and....Kind were Daddy's hands,
Hard....as....Steel were Daddy's hands,
When his children needed chastised as he saw it
he exercised his parenting skills.
with his hands.....

Daddy worked hard through all his years,
with his hands.....
Daddy worked long days at various jobs tearless
to feed, clothe and house his family,
with his hands.....

Daddy also worked hard religiously,
with his hands.....
Rebuilding his home that was burned tirelessly.
Never once complaining about his broken,
twisted fingers, still able to hold a token
with pain in his hands....

When it came time to plow, seed the soil,
or carefully fix something broken of his children,
grandchildren, friend or neighbor with out toil
with skilled hands.....

Daddy's hands were in greeting, or leaving
his presence with love if you cared
to stop and feel his grip long enough,
with your hands.....

There was a quiet straight gleam in his eyes
saying, "I CARE..I LOVE...FEEL MY HANDS".
.......I DID......DID YOU ?

OH !!! YES, DADDY WAS A MARINE
RIGID....and STEADFAST in many ways
as a Marine is taught to endure
with steel in his hands....

Soft was his heart, yet bursting with silent love.
You would never see him raging war on the highways.
The skill of his professional grip was secure
with his hands.....

Now, I salute you, Daddy with my hand,
and bid you peace on your final journey your way.
Live on in Love...Dad, Daddy, Grandpa, and friend.

Author's Comments:
"I witnessed my wife and her brothers grief over
their loss of a generous, special person their Dad."

# LEGACY OF LOVE

To all family, friends and loved ones

What shall I leave?
Maybe a few tokens will please
A gentle loving kiss
I hope you will never miss

I know...A poem
No, a book of my poems
2006,Copywrite @ Plantation
Short and sweet to all nations

Poems shall be amended
From the heart always intended
This way we shall be forever united
My love for all then never blighted

Roads traveled in different poem form
For all to read and enjoy
This to read rather than mourn
The stark reality when I'm gone

Author's Comments:

*"No, I am not dying. I have penned this in love as a thought for all of us what type of legacy shall we each leave. Then do it..."*

# Child In Tears

*To all Mothers and Daughters*

MOMMA, MOMMA

MY

PONY

TAIL

IS

TOO

TIGHT

Author's Comments:

*"I remember my daughter weeping
while having her hair done quickly for school.
How many of you can relate to this experience?"*

# CHAPTER 4. FRIENDSHIPS

# CLICKING THE KEYS

To all my fellow poet friends


Night and day click
Every day and night click
I feel sometimes like throwing a brick
Refreshed then back to the click

Never wanting a thought to lose
For quickly again I hear the click
I hope today I wont get a crick
In my neck or a touch of the blues

Almost finished new poem
Short and sweet this write
Need to go outside it is so bright
No more clicking I am out to roam


Author's Comments:
*"Just having fun before enjoying the Sunshine today."*

# Peace And Joy

*Questions of two little boys.*

## THE RESIDENCE OF PEACE

How much is the value of Peace?
How do I acquire Peace?
Where might I find this residence to reside?
Will you be please be my guide?

I have been told that it is near the residence of Joy
I remember it is not far from here, said my friend
No, it is not like the yellow brick road
As we played together with a small toad

The beginning of Wisdom by two little boys
Will you be my friend for life?
Each exchanging and crossing their heart with vows
They swore together on their Boy Scout knife

That the path to Peace and Joy begins with Love
Let us be the first to tell the world that we like Jesus
and how He played as a little boy with a white dove
He said, only Peace, Love and Joy within Him

Author's Comments:

*"The world now needs little boys and girls to teach us how
to love again and bring Peace and Joy to each other with Love."*

# Velcro Arms (Free Verse)

*The feeling of love*

The sound of Velcro sticking
Connecting one strap to another
or the union of a larger piece
No matter what is the color

Your arms my beloved wife
Your arms my lovely children
Your arms my dearest friends'
Your arms are all stronger than Velcro

Velcro arms of fellow poets
Velcro arms of co-workers
Velcro arms of my neighbors
Velcro arms of a stranger

Let us all stick together
Until He gathers us all to Himself
Heading to the Eternal ball as we prance
hand in hand like Velcro there to dance

Author's Comments:

*"When in doubt know we are all connected in love, so love all."*

# CHAPTER 5. JOY

# SHE GLOWS

To the Angel who spreads Angel dust over me

## SHE GLOWS

She glows with love from above.
Her heart has been beaten, yet scarred over.
She has been pierced on the rocks of life.
Her feet are the sandals of love.

## SHE GLOWS

Look not a hair misplaced.
Have you seen her smile?
She walks besides you for a while.
Yet she is willing to go the extra mile.

## SHE GLOWS

She has arms to hold you tight and so dear.
She has legs to kick-start your rear.
She will not let you falter, she is all woman.
Why does she glow, she is SUNSHINE.


Author's Comments:
*"When you truly love you will see her face to face, your Sweetheart,*
*Mom,*
*Wife, Friend. They are God's rainbows to us men."*

# Fill My Arms

*To my beloved*

You fill my arms when we dance
A kiss I feel of your sweet lips
Then you to send me in a trance
with just the swaying of your hips

With you beloved I need not plead
You know and fill my pressing need
Your in my arms I take the lead
Upon your beauty then to feed

You and I to never part
for now you wear a band of gold
forever in each others heart
Our love to never then grow old

The newness of each morning sun
memories of our wedding day
for two united then as one
deep in our hearts true love to stay

Author's Comments:
*"My way of saying thanks and blessing my beloved
for all she has and continues to do for me."*

# CROSS MY HEART

*To my beloved with love*

Darling, it is only you
I am always thinking of
So true am I, I shall commit
to you this heart of love

Cross My Heart

I thrill to hear your voice
to kiss your smiling face
holding hands as we walk
in our own private space

Cross My Heart

Dancing in our dreams
A sign, in love we're gloved
my desire then to tell you
you are so very truly loved

Cross My Heart

Author's Comments:

*"There are many ways to make love and
holding hands and this just one of them."*

# PERFECT LIFE

I smile to think of days gone by,
and how my life was more than stressed
but then she came and caught my eye,
and from that day my life was blessed.

How do you thank someone like she,
who means the whole wide world to me?
I guess the only way I know.
to tell her how I love her so.

And so I tell her every day
no matter then what comes our way
we stand together man and wife
Oh aint this such a..... perfect life.

# Flying Auras (Free Verse)

*To separated lovers*

Beloved's soaring towards each other
Their desired destiny is to be entwined
Their auras always on the same flight pattern
seeking each others distant shore for bonding

Swifter than a speeding bullet
Their target evermore in sight
Never a miss, as their laughter begins
No words exchanged, but love ever present

Their auras also in flight during day hours
Night follows the same flight pattern
Again their auras commingle in late hours
Climaxing their anticipated heart's close delights

A subtle hint of each other's needs
now expressed at a high vibration level
Both now resting in the joy of togetherness
of their new heightened after glow auras

Author's Comments:

*"The warm glow of love is always present in thought,
and word when beloved's are apart for whatever reason."*

# Fun

*Seek and you shall find true Joy*


If it ain't fun,

Don't do it

Just long enough ….

To figure out it ain't

Fun, 'n stop it !


If what we're doing for
God isn't simple, easy and
fun, perhaps we're doing
something else


Author's Comments:
*"Not everything is what it seems at first glance
or experience to be fun or lasting joy."*

# Beautiful

*To the eye of the beholder*

PICTURE

TAKEN

WITHOUT

CAMERA

MIND'S

EYE

RECORDED

SCENE

Author's Comments:

*"No tape recorder needed or camera to see beauty
all around us of people, places and things."*

# CRAYON BOX (FREE VERSE)

*To the child within us all*


Life reveals all the awesome colors before us
All these colors never could be held in a crayon box

Do you behold all the natural color changes in leaves?
Green
Red
Orange

Look up and see the hues presented in the sky
Dark
Light
Pastel

A child's delight to first choose
One or many crayons to color
A beautiful slanted figure drawn
First color chosen, love red for Mom

Wow, my own box of 64 crayons
Mom, I broke one, my favorite, crying
I will sharpen both ends you will have two
What is your favorite crayon color?


Author's Comments:

*"A poet colors words with Peace, Love and Joy"*

# Things I Find Beautiful

FACES (Free Verse)

Have you seen, I have............

The face of a newborn baby.....
The face of a new Mom.........
The face of a new Dad.........
The face of Jesus..............

The face of newborn animals...
The face of new Spring flowers...
The face of smiling people .....
The face of heroes.......

The face of my beloved.....
The face of a happy child.....
The face of newlyweds......
The face of new grandparents...

The face of two lovers.......
The face of birthdays.......
The face of success.......
The face of a happy poet.....

Now you see my face, smiling on you :)

# Exercise In High Heels

*What you can do alone...well almost*

Spend time alone in high heels
Grasp the moment in delight
Challenge your inner self-talents
Dance all around and do reels

Swirling now pick up the pace
You will instantly feel taller
You will feel also slimmer
Move quickly with style and grace

More indulgent than neighborhood walks
No more on floor exercises with a ball
nor driving to your favorite mall
Choose your favorite red or black stilettos

The woman in me ready to cope, challenge and deal
Energy now at high peak, Hi Honey…lets dance !
Love my exercise time in heels you now make me reel
Red is my choice for tomorrows exercise

Author's Comments:

*"A dance of love for your enjoyment."*

# CHAPTER 6. HOPE

# WE WAIT

*For all those who wait, that their desires be granted*


We wait for birth
We wait for love
We wait for life
to reveal it's meaning
(No you can't have the cheat sheet_

We wait year by year
for prayers to be answered
We wait for new experiences
We wait for return experiences

We wait in line
and
We wait, we wait
and
We wait some more

We know waiting is the
Law of Life
We know waiting is the
Measure of Love

We wait for the love
of Jesus to take us home
We wait with bated breath
Are you waiting with me?


Author's Comments:
*"Waiting teaches us patience, wait if you can."*

# Weight Of A Tear Drop

*To those of us that can shed a tear without harden hearts.*

Oh, the weight of a teardrop,
heavy, light, joyful, or sad,
the bearer measures all.

Oh, they almost taste like sea salt.
Heavier than a butterfly wing,
yet they can make you sing.

Oh, the weight of 911 teardrops
are not forgotten, but weigh
heavy on our hearts forever.

Oh, Light One bear with me
as I shed a tear of joy because
of the laughter you brought to me.

Oh, faithful friend, lover, poet,
let me give you that, which is lasting,
a spiritual wiping of your eyes everlasting.

Author's Comments:

*"It is OK for little boys to cry."*

# Sweet And Sour

Life has many surprises and twists
Sometimes we are slapped on the wrists
Never taste by itself a sour lemon
Always add some sugar..Yum ..

Now we can have lemonade
Right after we have played
Young children desire to become of age
Time will declare them or us a Sage

Listen well children, young and old
Never be unkind, harsh or bold
Put sweet and sour salad dressing
On your creative colorful salad

Life may serve up a different mixture
Don't become someone else's fixture
Put your own dressing on your destiny of life
You will avoid all personal strife

Author's Comments:

*"Just a poem to realize how all of life is
inner related from different views."*

# CRACKERS

*Lovers needing crackers*


Crackers are dry

without some cheese

What is a kiss?

without a squeeze


Author's Comments:

*"Just having fun with my muse today."*

# Change Is Good

*To all: There is a time for everything*

When you are

reluctant

to

change

think

of the

Autumn colors

Author's Comments:

*"Sometimes we just have to wait till the right time
like nature does to show all it's glory."*

# CHAPTER 7.  HUMOROUS

# My Little Surprise

*To my beloved and her wants (humor)*

No more housemaid's knees
No more scrubbing floors
No more washing windows
No more any chores.

No more dusting furniture
or cleaning out the den
I've got a little gift for you
eyes shut, I'll tell you when.

No more sweeping steps
I think you've had your fill
you're going to love this little gift
though it means, another bill

Now open up your big eyes
I just knew you'd jump for joy
A lovely Swedish au par girl
now whose a ...clever boy....;-)


Author's Comments:
*"You just never know what you will get
when you ask for something, be specific."*

# Market Place

While shopping for weekly groceries
I was going down the taxable aisle
In search of rolls of toilet paper
I reached up high to a pile.

The toilet paper, stacked on a rack
don't squeeze the Charmin pack
TV commercials always point out
so I handled gently no flack.

Throwing it in the shopping trolley
my beloved behind me I thought,
I never bothered to look around,
and a lesson there I was taught.

The same time I said I am desperate
to have a pee, I quickly must go
when I heard a voice behind me
Sir, there's something you ought to know.

This sir is not your trolley
and as for you needing a pee,
I can see that you are desperate,
but why are you telling me.

Blushing and red from embarrassment
my beloved appeared on store floor
I told her the trouble I'd got myself in.
We all laughed like never before.


Author's Comments:
*"A true situation of maximum embarrassment
that happened to me recently."*

# Toilet Lid

*To: All family members of 2 or more in the household*

TOILET LID

Up

Down

Up

Down

Up

Down dear

Yes, dear

## Author's Comments:

*"Bathroom dilemma, decisions, decisions"*

# CHAPTER 8. SPECIAL OCCASION

# Golden Love (Acrostic)

*To my Beloved and all my Poet friends*

Golden is this love I have for you,
Only you, can do the things you do
Little things that make me want to sing,
Darling, such joy, does your love bring.
Epitome, of everything pure.
Now strong our love, of this, I'm sure.

Likeness in spirit and soul, you and I,
Our God of Love, looks down, from high
Victory, the angels applaud,
Eternity bound our love and God.

# NAME YOUR COLORS

I have chosen Red, White and Blue
Red for the blood of our fallen true
White for the purity of their souls
Blue for the ultimate healing received

These colors are of my country's flag
American flag colors will never run or fade
Stood the test of time when called to be battled
Steadfast were these bravest never rattled

United we stand in homage to their heroism
Undaunted when asked to make supreme sacrifice
Unblemished the unfurled flag for patriotism
Until another fallen is called to be a star in our flag

Resting amongst all the very best we salute
Hands over our hearts remembering sons taken
Sound of taps for them and for freedom not forsaken
They did not run for freedom still rings and reigns

# CHAPTER 9.  CURRENT EVENTS

# SHORTCUTS

Icons all over my screen
Click me each one cries
No, click me first, wait …
One Icon missing at the gate

Where did it go?
I will search inward
Type in keyword…Poets
Now it is searching

Found, lost Icon
Do you want it sent to >
Yes, to my desktop
All shortcuts accounted for again

All Icons accounted for today
Search again for screen saver
Keyword…Picture of beloved
Found, I am happy again

# Chapter 10. Sensual

# Setting The Stage

*To those that yearn for a perfect evening*

Scented candles I have to light
In darkened room to glow they must
Choicest of wine chilled reflecting the glow
Glasses sparkle with red delight

Soft music turn on and down low
A chocolate wrapped delight upon the pillows
A second afterward comforting sweetness
Getting closer to being prepared.

Oh yes, bed sheets folded back
Nothing to harm or anything to be in way
Chilled, a blanket for my dearest
For under the sheets, I am warm

Walking into the room together
Prepared for a feast we are of each other
Such a vision to behold in anticipation
Oooops, place do not disturb sign on door

I wonder what goes on behind close doors
So new this love, yet prepared am I
Handle with loving care is our love motto
CAUTION I AM HOT! NOW CONTENTED..Nite Love

Author's Comments:
*"For those who have active imaginations,
I thought I would WET your appetite a bit."*

# Shall We Dance (First Pillow Fight)

To the dreamer that still is dancing

I asked her," Shall we dance?"
She looked at me like in a trance
"Yes, please take me to the floor"
Shoes off we glided near the door

I took the precious Darling
Spinning around so gracefully
We had danced before in dreams,
This time now in reality

Closer to the bedroom door
Feet lighter now they danced,
Anticipation quickly mounting,
Wondering best way to advance

Sunshine Darling, I asked
"Shall we", she replied," I guess"
The pillow fight began, I'm sacked
The winners prize, she on top, "YES".

Author's Comments:

*"A dreamer delight when at last two lovers fulfilled their heart's desires."*

# Pillow Fight (Second Continued)

The thrill of victory and the agony of defeat

Request to have a rematch
Best two out of three rounds
Winner takes all this time
Pillow fight now abounds

ROUND ONE: walls echoing pants
Heard to a magnitude of delight
Bed rocking with duel participants
Swings pillows loving fight

ROUND TWO: begins on knees
More aggressive they became
Faces flushed with exhaustion
Sound of the bell ending game

ROUND THREE: now rolling over
Upon sheet a mess the bed
I can't go on I cried
Stopping then our playtime fed

Glistening looks in her eyes
Saddened and dark were mine
She said, "NOW LET US DINE"
I said, "YOU'VE TOUCHED THIS HEART OF MINE"

GLEEFULLY OUR NEEDS TO MEET
As thong whipped off under the sheet
She," whispered this could be a ball
3 times a week, that's my call".

"WHAT STAMINA " she exclaimed!!
To be continued.....

Author's Comments:
*"Upon the bed of desires fun can be had between lovers."*

# Intimacy (Final Pillow Fight 3rd Round)

To all loving poets who enjoy loving
A Sunshine parched waterless land
A drink of fresh water
Brings forth desert flowers
A taste be it a drop or showers
Loving passionate words fall raining
Refreshing, exciting wetness flows
To kindred spirits beginning to soar
Dreaming of heights to fly and glow
Falling upon a heart of a poet
To another poet moisture from above
What a gift from a soaring Dove
Bringing new life to a parched Muse
Pillow fights new engagement rules
No shoes, no socks to hinder movement
Nude to the waist to be unencumbered
Winner takes all again as desired
Hitting high, hitting low were blows
Received with a loving glance
Knowing my turn is coming next
On her back falling way below
Is the end coming soon, she's hopeful
Difficult to move freely with liquid
Flowing in anticipation of penetration
Singing hearts mentally now agreeing
We have fought long and hard
My swelling tells me it is time
Shall we call it a draw? "YES"
Both winners now taking positions
Beneath and on top bodies shared
Like desires, let the reversal begin
In the ejaculation downloading state
His rain of love descending within.
PILLOW FIGHTS ARE OVER
BOTH WINNERS TOOK ALL.
Author's Comments:
*"A fun time was had by all and I hope you enjoy
all in the spirit of love and Sunshine."*

# Chapter 11. Other

# Junk

*What is on your dresser?*

THIS
- N -
THAT


STUFF


ODDS
- N -
ENDS


Author's Comments:

*"A rambling mind created this.*
*No rhyme or reason just having fun*
*sharing allowed if you dare?"*

# The Eyes Have It

*To the eyes that watch at night*

CONSUMED

Among the forest

he dwells at night.

Only the eyes of the owl

are not totally at rest.

His eyes are seen searching

then darting in flight

to his prey now to be

CONSUMED

Author's Comments:

*"Careful when walking in the forest at night.
Be still and you shall see how the hungry feed themselves."*

# What Is Your Opinion On Bed Wetting?

*To all those little boys and girls who have suffered this trauma*

Crying I awake from another nightmare
With fear I tremble...I hear mom about
The same stench and wetness in the air
He's done it again...I hear her shout

Changed sheets, beating, I feel pain
Showering, crying, red eyes blamed on soap
Fresh now, off to school, oh no late again!
English Teacher kind and gives me hope

End of school day, teacher smiles lovingly
Skipping home smiling, the kind things she said
Enter back door but greeted harshly,
Homework, chores done, then off to bed

I pray to the Lord upon my knees
To help me overcome this awful dread
Can mother not see it's her cruelty
That makes me keep wetting the bed

This all happened a long time ago
But the memory is ever clear
A child's reason for wetting the bed
Is often associated with fear.

Author's Comments:
*"Be not afraid for the Lord will deliver you from all that pains you."*

# Six Saturdays In A Week (Free Verse)

*To those wanting more retirement free time*
SIX SATURDAYS

TODAY is the first of six Saturdays
Out in the yard to pick up sticks
Spread weed killer on lawn
Take the dog for a walk

TODAY is the second of six Saturdays
Mow the grass and clip the shrubs
Exercise and swimming day
Spend time with wife

TODAY is the third of six Saturdays
Weed and water the flowerbeds
Compose a poem or two
Rocking chair memory time day

TODAY is the fourth of six Saturdays
Clean and wash the vehicles
Time to get oil changed
Fill up the vehicle with Petro

TODAY is the fifth of six Saturdays
Getting tired, hard work this week
Must visit shut-ins
Good love movie on tonight

TODAY is the sixth of six Saturdays
Market place and mail packages
Visit children, grandchildren
Play and travel day

SUNDAY is the Lord's Day.
Every day is a Saturday when retired
No rush to get all chores done on one
Saturday, there are always six more
Saturdays waiting for you.

Author's Comments:
*"Retirement hopes and dreams of the good life for many
and the activities awaiting them. Enjoy each day.
No more rushing to get all these chores done on one Saturday. One
day at a time."*

# The Thumb Rules

To: All decision makers


Shall I extend my thumb?
Two rules that always apply

Extend upward means one thing
Lower downward means another
Decisions

One could mean life
Another could mean death
Decisions

A thumb to grasp an object
A thumb to release an object
Decisions

Many uses for the thumb
Many rules apply to each
Double thumbs up or down
Decisions

A rule of thumb is 80/20
80 for you, 20 for me
20 for you, 80 for me
Decisions


Author's comments:

What rule of thumb and numbers
do you follow?

# Selection 2
# Cinquain Contents

# Section 2 Cinquains

"Cinquain:  a Form consisting of 5 lines,
and has a required number of syllables, and a specific topic.
Line 1:  title (noun)-2 syllables
Line 2:  Description-4 syllables.
Line 3:  Action-6 syllables.
Line 4:  Feeling (phrase) 8 syllables
Line 5:  Title (synonym for title) – 2 syllables."

CINQUAIN  (Example)

Few words
Any subject
Not many rules to learn
Right syllable count important
Good Luck

Author's Comments:
"Cinquain 2/4/6/8/2"

## Hot Love

Warm touch
sets heart on fire
flames then dance and flicker
igniting passion deep inside
Hot Love

## Fever

Fever
Your hot kisses
melt me when they touch mine
knees instantly buckle from heat
Hot love

## Song Bird

Sweet sound
my love singing
like nightingale in spring
together we make sweet music
Duet

## My Love

My love
In love with you
Words not always needed
Eyes speak a thousand words... goody..
Bed time

# FEELINGS

Feelings
True sensations
Experienced through touch
Thoughts imagination and need
Heartfelt

# OUR LOVE

Our love
Smooth as satin
Fragrant as a blossom
Warm as a brand new morning sun
Worshipped

# PERFUME

Perfume
her special scent
stimulating effect
keeps her forever close to me
fragrant

# LOVES TOUCH

Loves touch
moist hot feelings
over ride the arid
night air as we gently caress
and melt

## LOVE

Within
The eyes of your
Beloved, You will see
the reflection of your own soul
True love

## TIME

My time
with you, treasured
your time with me. I'm blessed
forever, us making good time
as one

## My Goals

My goals
short term, long term
all goals have now been met
for you my beloved were both
achieved

## Colors

Colors
Shades of your eyes
found in the morning skies
your lips the softest loving pink
Perfect

# CHAPTER 2. INSPIRATION

# Muse

My Muse
encouraging
source of inspiration
that inspires creativity
spellbound

# His Light

Each day
walk tall and proud
In heaven's divine light
Teach others that they may also
know God

# Angel

Angel
A beautiful
messenger of the Lord
that protects and offers guidance
Divine

# Happy

Happy
always smiling
walking on air because
love came and shone its light on us
Glowing

# My Lord

*To those desiring absolute Peace, Love and Joy*


JESUS
Is calling you
Will you welcome Him now
In your heart to remain always
Yes, Yes

# Jesus

JESUS
Jesus is Lord
Lord Jesus have mercy
Jesus Lord, Jesus Christ Thank you
Lord God

# CHAPTER 3. RELATIONSHIPS

# Daddy

Daddy
We love you so
and miss you when you go
so please, please hurry home from work
Your girls

# Mistrust

Mistrust
A lack of trust
Arising from a lack of
confidence due to suspicion
Unsure

# Children

Children
Gods little Gifts
To love and cherish them
and forever to keep them safe
from harm.

# Daughter

Daughter
my pride and joy
as sweet as an angel
you mean the whole wide world to me
Dad's Girl

# Surname

Sons two

Proud same surname

My pride and joy, loving

Outstanding husbands, now parent

Dad's gift

# Button

Who is
Brightest button
Mums special button box
Because my light blue eyes sparkle
I am

# CHAPTER 4. FRIENDSHIP

# Friendship

Reach out
to mankind and
realize that much more
can be accomplished with hand of
friendship

# Anger

Anger
Displeases me
Feelings of frustration
Life is too short for arguments
All Friends?

# CHAPTER 5. JOY

# Feet

Bare feet
imprints in sand
Leaves trail across the beach
paddle in warm ocean water
Feet clean

# My Luck

My Luck
Preparation
Is opportunity
Given responsibility
New Job

# CHAPTER 6. HOPE

# Reiki

Reiki
For well being
and spiritual growth
Enhances quality of life
Healing

# Healing

Hands on Spiritual
Channeling healing
Universal life energy
Reiki

# No Time

No time
To love me now
No time for you either
Too busy to love, email works
Right time

# Waiting Room

On time
People waiting
Doctor visit, hurting
Double booked now, two hours to wait
My turn

# CHAPTER 7. HUMOROUS

# SMILE

Smiling
You are happy
Smile and people smile back
Makes for a much happier world
Say cheese

# SMOKING

Smoking
said to stunt growth
then am I truly glad
I never took up the habit
Wink, Wink

# Vanishing Cream

How come
pot is empty
and that you are still here
Never understand woman's world
Give up

# Singing

My voice
Too loud and deep
Family turns deaf ear
All smile without hearing? Ho, ho
Ear plugs

# Ring

Cell phone
Vibrator ring
Annoying always on
Hello Honey, Yes I love you
Drop call

# Circus

Circus
Entertainment
Acrobats clowns jugglers
Traveling company performs
Big Top

# Flashlight

Comic
Now flashlight on
Under the sheets hiding
Stop laughing now, mom will hear us
Reading

# Falsies

Falsies
New pearlie whites
Like stars come out at night
They are soaking till morning light
False teeth

# Remote

Now Poised
Remote in hand
Couch potato with drink
Decisions, sports, news, or movie
Sleeping

# CHAPTER 8. NATURE

# Nature

Nature
primitive state
of beauty untouched by
the hand of greed and destruction
God's Gifts

# Water

Liquid
Clear colorless
Odorless and tasteless
Essential for maintaining life
Fluid

# Raining

Raining
feet getting wet
now I am in trouble
forgot to empty the bucket
roof leaks

# Flowers

Flowers
cultivated
for their blooms and blossoms
fragrant colorful and showy
scented

# Making Waves

Kicking
Splashing, gliding
Stroking, thrashing, moving
Aqua diamonds glistening
Swimming

# CHAPTER 9.  SEASONAL

# Mower

Mower
Red, dual blades
Repair or fix daily
Nearly new, belt driven, gas hog
Broken


# Summer

Summer
Sun is so hot
Burns my flesh like your love
Different kind of heat is this
Scorching

# Easter

Easter
Chocolate eggs
Bonnets to parade in
Celebrating our dear sweet Lord
Amen

# Haunted

Haunted?
Loud squeaky noise
ghostly figure on stairs
Phew! Just Aunt Sally sleep walking
Freaky

# Springtime

Springtime
Buds bursting forth
Splendid colors on show
Spring cleaning jobs get underway
Clean sweep

# CHAPTER 10. SUPPORT

# All Things

All things
Come to those that
wait, I waited and I
found what I had been longing for
My dream

# My Life

My life
Filled with such joy
Reason so very clear
as you stand here in front of me
My world

# Tidiness

Mom shouts
Tidy your room
Make orderly and neat
Clothes soiled on floor, room still messy
Help Mom

# CHAPTER 11. ANIMALS

# Watch Dog

Watch Dog
Neck tethered tight
Bark bigger than his bite
Beware of dog, big joke, all show
Best friend

# Spider

Eight legs
Traps flies in web
Clever little spinners
Arachnid and not an insect
Scary

# MERMAID

Lady
Immersed with fish
Guardian upon rocks
Cool water encased figurine
Fish Tank

# PEACOCK

Plumage
Strutting all hues
Belongs to Paradise
He has stiff self important gait
Proud bird

# CHAPTER 12. FOOD

# Donuts

Donuts
Sugar, sugar
Now with coffee, tea, milk
Filling or glazed a yum delight
Dunkin

# Buttered Toast

My toast
I love buttered
Raisin or cinnamon
Favorite marmalade, jelly
Your choice

# WIGGLE

Wiggle
Shiver, shimmer
Light, smooth, cool, colorful
Tastefully pleasing to palate
Jell "O"

# RECIPE

New test
Chef only knows
We are the Guinea Pigs
Mysterious ingredients
Pot luck

# Dessert

Dessert
Just a small taste
But I always want more
Forget calories and enjoy
Sweet tooth

# Nutrition

Menu
For healthy life
Now follow directions
Eat fresh veggies, fruit, fish, turkey
Slimming

## COFFEE

Sniff sniff
Great aroma
Teasing my taste buds
Special "Sneek A Diddle" coffee
Great Brand

## LICKING

Treat day
Tastefully cool
Yum, Yum two scoops for each
Choices chocolate or vanilla
Ice cream

# CHAPTER 13. CURRENT EVENTS

# Open

Open
An open mind
has more power than large
guns or many a tight clenched fist
Peace Please

# Petroleum

Fuel
Bad gas prices
Jesse James used a gun
Oil cartels use cash registers
Robbers

# Chapter 14. Special Occasions

## Shaved Legs

Shaved legs
New cut and scrapes
Smooth as silk with lotion
Perfumed with the choicest of scents
Dance night

## Kicking

Kicking
Splashing, gliding
Stroking, thrashing, moving
Aqua diamonds glistening
Swimming

# CHAPTER 15. AMUSING

# My Teacher

Fifth grade
Teacher's vision
Caught chewing and cracking
Distraught now no recess today
Spit gum

# Annoying Messages

Hello
Important call
Please contact me, you WON!
Mr. A. Fake Telemarketer
Good bye

# CHAPTER 16. PROFESSIONAL

# Nurses

Nurses
Same height, same build
Same blue eyes, same blond hair
Special nurses caring for all
Angels

# Firemen

Firemen
Our great hero's
Men giving of themselves
Dedicated to our safety
Saves lives

## Investments

Stocks, bonds
Your loss, my gain
Day Trader investors
Stock market fear and greed driven
Money

## Poet

Poet
Write to express
Feelings and emotions
Pictures painted with many words
A gift

# CHAPTER 17.  POETS

# Author

Author
writer of books
or any other text
one who writes as a profession
creates

# Poet

Write to express
Feeling and emotions
Pictures painted with many words
A gift

# CHAPTER 18.  GAMES

# PLAY BALL

PLAY BALL
My turn to bat
Little league glove and ball
Now the All Star game has begun
Home run

# GAME ON

Game on
Now get ready
My scissors, rocks, paper
Scissors cuts the paper, I win
My turn?

# CHAPTER 19. OTHER

# TRAFFIC

Traffic
The passage of
people or vehicles
along routes of transportation
Mobile

# FLASHES

Flashes
Now hot again
Men don't understand me
Everyday never knowing when
It sucks

# Ego

Ego
I dodge the truth
Self thinks it knows it all
Covers my fear of rejection
Heartfelt

# Umbrella

Brolly
Protects from rain
Circular canopy
Collapsible and portable
Keep dry

# South Wales

South Wales
The Land of song
Valleys and mountains high
Daffodil and leek the emblems
Celtic

# Cinquain

Few words
Any subject
Not many rules to learn
Right syllable count important
Good Luck

Author's Comments:
*"Cinquain 2/4/6/8/2"*

# About The Poet/Author

*As a gifted poet, James Pocza is sharing his vision of life experiences for you to enjoy. He gleaned an understanding, depth, and awareness of many moments in his life, inspiring him to write this book of poems.*

*While attending Stark State College he wrote, edited and appeared in a public relations program promoting Stark State College. He is a charter member of Toastmasters International and a Advanced Toastmaster Speaker. A founding member of www.Poets.com, and also a member of www.worldofpoetry.com. James is a Human and Social Services graduate, a Spiritual Director, a Reiki Master/Teacher, a Businessman and a US Army Veteran.*

*James, is a graduate of Stark State College, Canton, Ohio, a graduate of Television Workshop School, Cleveland, Ohio, attended Cleveland State University and Kent State University.*

*Happily married, blessed with children and grandchildren, James and Jeanne live in a small community in Ohio. He continues to study and write poetry.*

*Visit James's web site, www.reikienergycenter.com*
*tapestrypoems@aol.com*

Printed in the United States
71492LV00001B/1-99